FIRST SOURCE TO
GYMNASTICS

RULES, EQUIPMENT, AND KEY ROUTINE TIPS

by Tracy Nelson Maurer

Consultant:
Paige Roth
Owner, Iowa Gym-Nest
Region IV Xcel Chair

CAPSTONE PRESS
a capstone imprint

First Facts are published by Capstone Press,
1710 Roe Crest Drive, North Mankato, Minnesota 56003
www.mycapstone.com

Library of Congress Cataloging-in-Publication Data
Names: Maurer, Tracy, 1965- author.
Title: First Source to Gymnastics : Rules, Equipment, and Key Routine
Tips /By Tracy Nelson Maurer.
Description: North Mankato, Minnesota : An imprint of Capstone Press, 2018. |
Series: First Facts. First Sports Source | Includes bibliographical
references and index. | Audience: Age 7-9. | Audience: K to Grade 3.
Identifiers: LCCN 2016059570| ISBN 9781515769453 (library binding : alk. paper) |
ISBN 9781515769477 (pbk. : alk. paper) | ISBN 9781515769491 (ebook pdf : alk. paper)
Subjects: LCSH: Gymnastics—Juvenile literature.
Classification: LCC GV461.3 M324 2018 | DDC 796.44—dc23
LC record available at https://lccn.loc.gov/2016059570

Editorial Credits
Bradley Cole, editor; Sarah Bennett and Katy LaVigne, designers; Eric Gohl, media researcher;
Kathy McColley, production specialist

Photo Credits
Alamy Stock Photo: Aflo Co., Ltd., 17; Dreamstime: Saltcityphotography, cover; iStockphoto:
Tassii, 15; Newscom: EFE/Javier Etxezarreta, 6 (right); Shutterstock: 4Max, 1 (background, top
right), Air Images, 4, ITALO, 1, 11 (left), Leonard Zhukovsky, 5, 19, 21, Lilyana Vynogradova, 6
(left), 11 (right), Luigi Fardella, 13, Mitrofanov Alexander, 7 (right), roibu, cover (background), 1
(background, top left & middle), Sasha Samardzija, 9, testing, 7 (left)

Design Elements: Shutterstock

Printed and bound in China.
004610

TABLE OF CONTENTS

Gymnastics Fun

Running! Jumping! Flipping! Gymnastics is full of action. Girls and boys around the world join gymnastics clubs. They build strength and learn flexibility and balance. Many have dreams of winning an Olympic gold medal someday. Do you dream of being a gymnast?

"I kind of do think of myself as a superhero and just flying high, and doing these crazy flips."

–Gabby Douglas,
U.S. Olympic gold medalist

5

Types of Gymnastics

ARTISTIC GYMNASTICS

Artistic gymnastics have been part of the Olympics since the first competition in 1896. Women's events include the vault, uneven bars, balance beam, and floor exercise. Men's events are the vault, floor exercise, pommel horse, still rings, parallel bars, and horizontal bar.

TRAMPOLINE AND TUMBLING

All gymnasts learn basic tumbling moves, including the somersault. Some gymnasts advance to trampoline, power tumbling, **synchronized** trampoline, and double mini-trampoline events. Trampolining became an Olympic sport in 2000.

RHYTHMIC GYMNASTICS

Rhythmic gymnasts perform routines to music. They compete in five events. Each event uses different props, including a rope, a hoop, a ball, clubs, and ribbon. Rhythmic gymnastics was added to the Summer Olympics in 1984.

ACROBATIC GYMNASTICS

Shows such as Cirque du Soleil and cheerleading competitions often show high-energy **acrobatics**. Acrobatic gymnastics compete in groups or pairs. Events include pairs, mixed pair, women's group, and men's group.

synchronized—when two or more people perform the same movements at the same time

acrobatics—movements borrowed from gymnastics, such as handstands, flips, and forward rolls

7

CHAPTER 1
Geared Up

Gymnastic club gyms have mats, bars, rings, and other equipment. Club gyms are safe places to learn and practice skills. Gymnasts use a specific piece of equipment or **apparatus** to perform certain skills. They do flips off a **vaulting table**. They practice moves and exercises with the rings.

HORSE VAULTING HISTORY

Vaulting traces its history to ancient Rome. Roman warriors jumped onto wooden horses to practice jumping onto real horses.

apparatus—equipment used in gymnastics, such as the balance beam or uneven bars

vaulting table—an apparatus for launching a gymnast into the air to perform flips and twists

9

What to Wear

Gymnasts wear snug clothing that won't catch on equipment. Girls wear one-piece **leotards** for competitions and practices. They may also wear shorts over the leotards at practices.

Boys wear shorts and T-shirts at practices. They compete in a one-piece **singlet** with shorts or pants over it. Teams usually compete in matching uniforms.

WHAT NOT TO WEAR TO COMPETITIONS

At competitions, gymnasts may lose points if they wear:
- a T-shirt
- a headband, cape, or scarf
- jewelry (Stud earrings are allowed.)
- leotard straps less than 0.75 inches (2 centimeters) wide

leotard—a snug and stretchy, one-piece uniform worn by female gymnasts and dancers

singlet—a stretchy, sleeveless one-piece uniform for male gymnasts

CHAPTER 2

Form and Routines

Gymnasts try to keep their bodies in certain forms or shapes when they perform. Toes curve downward. Ankles stay together most of the time.

The mat is for practicing. Beginners learn rolls, tucks, and cartwheels. After gymnasts learn basic skills, they try more difficult tricks. They perform a series of tricks called a **routine** at competitions. Good form and a bit of flair leads to higher scores.

HOW LONG?

Some routines last more than 1 minute. The floor routine is up to 90 seconds of nonstop action. Other events, such as the vault, take just 6 or 7 seconds. All routines need hours of practice.

routine—a series of tricks linked one after another
in a performance on one apparatus

Practice

Gymnasts train with coaches at gyms to learn new skills. They do push-ups, sit-ups, and other exercises to build upper body and core strength. Exercises such as jumping jacks or jumping rope increase **stamina**.

FUEL YOUR BODY!

Gymnasts need good fuel! Eat balanced meals with plenty of lean proteins, whole grains, and dairy foods. Healthy snacks include yogurt, a bran muffin, or oatmeal.

14

stamina—the energy and strength to keep doing something for a long time

CHAPTER 3

Rules of the Sport

Judges watch for smooth and strong movements. Jumps and vaults with great height and distance earn good scores. Judges expect landings without wobbles too.

The Junior Olympics scoring starts gymnasts with a score of 10.0. Points are subtracted for mistakes, such as missing requirements and other errors.

TRICK NAMES

New tricks are often named for the first gymnast to perform it at a worldwide competition. Kurt Thomas is known for the Thomas Flair. It is a spinning move done with the legs held in a V shape. He first performed this move in 1977 in Barcelona, Spain.

"When I began my career, I just wanted to do cartwheels."

–Romanian Olympian *Nadia Comaneci, in* Letters to a Young Gymnast

NADIA COMANECI

FACT

Romanian Nadia Comaneci achieved the first perfect score in women's gymnastics at the Olympics in 1976 in Montreal, Canada.

If you dream of competing in the Olympics, you should join a gym that trains **elite** gymnasts. Only elite gymnasts may compete at the national and international level. With practice, skill, and determination, your dreams can come true!

2016 OLYMPICS

FACT
Gymnasts must turn 16 in the calendar year to compete in the Olympics.

elite—describes gymnasts who are among the best

ELITE COMPETITION SCORING

Difficulty Score (D) + Execution Score (E) = Final Score (F)

D scores start at 0 and increase with points for performing each difficult skill.

E scores start at 10 and decrease with errors.

CHAPTER 4

Performance Tips

Great gymnasts like Simone Biles make their routines look easy. They shine with confidence. But they have fallen countless times along the way. What's their secret to success? They learn from their falls and practice even harder.

TIPS AND TRICKS

- Slippery hands? Try chalk powder on your hands—and maybe even your feet!

- When you fall, tuck and roll in the direction you're already moving. Cross your arms over your chest to prevent injuries to your fingers, wrists, or elbows.

- Practice your landings. Bend your knees when you hit the mat. Hold your arms out straight with your palms down for extra balance.

- Strike a final pose with straight legs, arched back, chin up, and arms high. Smile with gold-medal confidence!

"Before I begin a routine I just think 'confidence' and how many times I've done this routine."

–Simone Biles

21

Glossary

acrobatics (AK-ruh-bat-iks)—movements borrowed from gymnastics, such as handstands, flips, and forward rolls

apparatus (a-puh-RA-tuhs)—equipment used in gymnastics, such as the balance beam or uneven bars

elite (i-LEET)—describes gymnasts who are among the best

leotard (LEE-uh-tard)—a snug and stretchy, one-piece uniform worn by female gymnasts and dancers

routine (roo-TEEN)—a series of tricks linked one after another in a performance on one apparatus

singlet (SING-let)—a stretchy, sleeveless one-piece uniform for male gymnasts

stamina (STAM-uh-nuh)—the energy and strength to keep doing something for a long time

synchronized (SING-kruh-nized)—when two or more people perform the same movements at the same time

vaulting table (VAWL-ting TAY-buhl)—an apparatus for launching a gymnast into the air to perform flips and twists

Read More

Capucilli, Alyssa Satin. *My First Gymnastics Class.* Ready-to-Read. New York: Simon Spotlight, 2016.

Gray, Karlin. *Nadia: The Girl Who Couldn't Sit Still.* Boston: Houghton Mifflin Harcourt, 2015.

Mattern, Joanne. *Simone Biles: America's Greatest Gymnast.* Rookie Biographies. New York: Children's Press An Imprint of Scholastic Inc., 2017.

Internet Sites

FactHound offers a safe, fun way to find Internet sites related to this book. All of the sites on FactHound have been researched by our staff.

Here's all you do:
Visit www.facthound.com
Type in this code: 9781515769453

 **Super-cool stuff!** Check out projects, games and lots more at
www.capstonekids.com

Index